Agile Governance and Audit

An overview for auditors and agile teams

Agile Governance and Audit

An overview for auditors and agile teams

CHRISTOPHER WRIGHT

IT Governance Publishing

IT Governance Publishing
IT Governance Limited
Unit 3, Clive Court
Bartholomew's Walk
Cambridgeshire Business Park
Ely
Cambridgeshire
CB7 4EA
United Kingdom

www.itgovernance.co.uk

First published in the United Kingdom in 2014
by IT Governance Publishing.

ISBN 978-1-84928-587-2

FOREWORD

Why am I writing this book?

A very good question and one I have often asked myself in the middle of the night when the blank page beckoned and deadlines loomed. Then I realised writing a book is very much like running or auditing a project. When you start out you have an idea what you will end up with, but you cannot be certain of the final product. It's exciting, challenging and you hope it will produce something useful and worthwhile. At the same time it can also be scary and alarming; daunting even when you look at the task ahead.

I am writing it because I can and no one else has. I have been involved in IT projects and get tired of seeing the same mistakes repeated. Typical scenarios are systems that do not meet user requirements, poor testing, no evidence of decisions made or why they were made. Someone once described it to me as everyone 're-inventing square wheels'. Another symptom is audits of projects are completed late with recommendations that are expensive to implement and add little business value.

Over the last ten years or so, the dichotomy between projects and audit has increased. Project managers are under increasing pressure to produce more with less. The pace of change is relentless, with technological opportunities way beyond what we imagined even a decade ago. At the time of writing 'Big Data' and 'Bring Your Own Device' are key trends – but these will quickly be replaced by something else. At the height of the 'dot-com' boom it was generally believed that you had only 30 days to get a new idea to market – otherwise someone else would be in the same space. Many projects I have worked on in recent years were virtually out of date before they were finished. At the same time we have seen pressures in corporate governance. Failures such as Enron and WorldCom led to the Sarbanes-Oxley Act in the US. This has had global impacts in the way we view corporate control, including controls required in systems for financial reporting and the way that changes are made to these systems.

I get so frustrated seeing good project teams fail because they do not understand the need for proper governance and control. Some auditors also fail to understand the pressures on the project team and the significance and impact of business drivers during projects.

There is a better way. The issues are as much cultural as technical or management based. Auditors' views of project teams are often summarised in a recent remark I had from an auditor: 'Ah, Agile – that's some wild project approach hippy types dreamt up when they had smoked too much wacky backy.'

Project teams, if they think of auditors at all, probably consider the following definition to be apt:

'The typical auditor is a man past middle age, spare, wrinkled, intelligent, cold, passive, non-committal with eyes like cod fish: polite in contact, but at the same time unresponsive, calm and as damnably composed as a concrete post or a plaster of Paris cast: Human petrifaction with a heart of feldspar and without charm – minus bowels, passion or a sense of humour. Happily they never re-produce and all of them go to Hell.' Elbert Hubbard, 1900.

In reality most auditors I know only fit some of the preceding criteria! They generally have a more positive approach to helping the organisations that they work for, seeing themselves as a vital part of ensuring corporate governance but also adding business and commercial benefit. Since I started looking at Agile audit a few years ago there has been a growing interest in the subject from auditors. A number of audit teams are even looking at Agile techniques and tools to plan and undertake their own audit work.

One reason for my writing this book is that I am a creative thinker who wants to see technology used for the benefit of the business. I am also a middle-aged, wrinkled, qualified auditor. I can see both points of view and seek a consensus (in true Agile fashion) between these two very extreme views.

Everyone involved in a project wants a good outcome. By improving our understanding of one another we can interact better for the benefit of our own careers as well as the project in progress. We are all intelligent beings and (although it's hard to believe on projects sometimes!) responsible, professional adults.

To auditors the introduction of Agile can be frightening as it represents a completely different approach to the ones they are used to. The use of Agile for non-IT projects such as Sarbanes-Oxley compliance, introducing new products, refurbishing retail outlets and even planning and running audits means that general auditors as well as IT specialist auditors are now coming into contact with Agile. For experienced auditors I want to show that they can adapt and re-use their audit skills they may have gained doing traditional waterfall, CCTA Risk Analysis and Management Method (CRAMM) or PRINCE2® audits to Agile. For less experienced auditors I want to encourage them to consider some of these good practices and their application to Agile audits.

So that's why I developed training courses for auditors and for project teams. It is also why I wrote this book. I also thought, like projects, it could be fun.

My aim has been to provide a book that is readable and of use to those with varying degrees of, or even no, project audit experience.

The Agile community is one of open sharing and seeking constant improvement. I hope my small offering in the form of this book contributes to that body of knowledge. But I do not have all the answers – indeed as an auditor I don't even have all the questions. I would welcome your thoughts and suggestions as to how auditors and Agile teams can work better together for the mutual benefit of the organisations we all work for and our own development (*see LinkedIn group details under Further Resources*).

PREFACE

This book provides an overview of Agile for auditors or other risk professionals who may not have encountered this approach before. It also provides a perspective for Agile teams on what auditors and risk professionals need as key stakeholders in a project and the sort of questions they are likely to ask.

It is based on my own opinions and experience. Some will read this book and disagree with some of these ideas, particularly if they have worked on different types of Agile projects to the ones I have been on. If I have generated some thought and discussion, I will have achieved my objective.

Each chapter includes some tips and hints for auditors so they can adapt their style of auditing for Agile. We will consider detailed audit requirements for each stage in the following chapters. For each main part of the process we will consider:

- What are the audit objectives?
- What are the business risks covered by this objective?
- What controls would we expect and how can these be audited?

The auditor should focus on both the controls over the governance and execution of the project, and the controls to be included in the final deliverable.

I have also included case studies for project initiation and high-level requirements to help you understand some of the practicalities of the issues raised.

ABOUT THE AUTHOR

A qualified accountant, Certified Information Systems Auditor® and Certified ScrumMaster®, Chris has more than 30 years' experience of providing financial and IT advisory and risk management services. He worked for 16 years at KPMG where he managed a number of major IS audit and risk assignments. These included a number of project risk and business control reviews. He was head of information risk training in the UK and also ran training courses overseas including India and Iceland. He has worked in a wide range of industry sectors including oil and gas, public sector and, aviation and travel.

For the past seven years he has been an independent consultant specialising in financial, Sarbanes-Oxley (SOX) and operational controls for major Enterprise Resource Planning (ERP) implementations at Oil and Gas enterprises. During this time he has seen a significant change from traditional to Agile project management. He has developed a number of techniques and tools to provide fit for purpose controls and governance frameworks within these revised approaches.

ACKNOWLEDGEMENTS

I would like to thank all of those individuals and organisations that have been brave enough to let me try new ideas and approaches. Some were successful, some were not, but all were learning opportunities.

This book would not have been possible without the help, encouragement and support of a number of people including my long-term friends and colleagues Mike Hughes, Janet Thorneycroft, Diane Hill, Mike Whelan and Colin Bezant. Also a special thank-you for the support and patience of my wife Amanda who unfortunately understands me very well. I am also grateful to the many Agile practitioners who have developed the thinking around this – and in many cases been open about their mistakes and failures so that others can learn and run their own projects even better.

My thanks also to Brian Johnson, CA, Chris Evans, ITSM specialist and Jamie Lynn Cooke, author of *Agile: An Executive Guide*, *Everything you want to know about Agile* and *The Power of the Agile Business Analyst* for their helpful comments during the review process.

As a Certified ScrumMaster I particularly acknowledge the work of the Scrum Alliance and the resources it makes available.

CONTENTS

Chapter 1: Introduction to Agile............................1
Overview..1
Agile's history...1
Agile definition...3
Agile Manifesto...5
Agile principles...10
Three pillars of control..11
Agile software development models..........................13
Conclusion...17
Chapter 2: Agile Versus Waterfall........................19
Overview..19
Comparing Agile with waterfall...............................19
How to audit Agile/waterfall decision.....................23
Conclusion...27
**Chapter 3: Why Doesn't My Auditor/Agile Project
Team Understand Me?**...29
Overview..29
Audit and Agile cultures..29
How can we have a successful audit?.......................33
Conclusion...34
Chapter 4: Project Initiation and Risk Assessment.....35
Overview..35
Project initiation..36
Risk assessment...38
How to audit project initiation................................41
Conclusion...44
Chapter 5: Case Study PID & Risk Assessment..........45
Overview..45
Case Study – extract of Project Initiation Document......46
Suggested response..48

Contents

Chapter 6: High-Level Requirements 51
Overview 51
Gathering of requirements 52
Including controls in requirements 55
How to audit requirements gathering 56
Conclusion 58
Chapter 7: Case Study for High-Level Requirements..59
Overview 59
Case Study - extract of requirements 59
Suggested response 63
Chapter 8: Building and Testing 67
Overview 67
Build phase 68
Testing phase 71
How to audit build and testing phases 74
Conclusion 75
Chapter 9: Handover to the Business 77
Overview 77
Release management 78
Business readiness 79
IT readiness 80
Controls readiness 81
Auditing business handover 83
Conclusion 84
Chapter 10: Documentation for Governance and Audit 87
Overview 87
Agile governance objectives and principles 87
Governance documentation 90
Audit of Agile governance 92
Conclusion 94
Chapter 11: Top Tips to Take-Away 95
Further Resources 97

CHAPTER 1: INTRODUCTION TO AGILE

Overview

Before we consider Agile governance and audit we need a common understanding of the history of Agile and how it is defined. The dictionary definition of Agile is 'nimble, mentally quick or acute'. The thesaurus adds words such as active, lively, prompt, quick, sharp and sprightly. These are not words usually associated with IT programmes and projects!

Many organisations have their own terminology and definitions – of varying accuracy and validity. This also causes some confusion, so throughout this book I rely upon the following widely accepted structures:

- Agile definition
- Agile Manifesto
- Agile principles
- Agile 3 pillars of control.

An understanding of these will enable the auditor to discuss the key issues, risks and controls for a project with the Agile project team in a practical and clear way. In this chapter we will look at the history of Agile before considering each of the preceding structures, and also look at some of the main types of Agile project.

Agile's history

The Agile approach did not start in the world of software and IT. Agile's origins are in engineering with the manufacturing practices that emerged in the Far East. Consumers have constant changes in needs and purchasing patterns and so businesses needed to adapt quickly to new product demands. We have also seen a rapid change in technology available to customers and manufacturers. The product development lifecycles available to suppliers were too long. All the work in developing a product or service could be quickly lost if a competitor came to market with a similar offering sooner. On the production side too there was increasing demand for Just-in-Time production, to reduce supply chain costs and the risk that components would be delivered for finished goods that would not be produced due to better versions being available.

For example, consider the rapid development changes of audio recording over the last 30 years. Various media have come and gone. Look at the length of time vinyl recordings were in use – and how quickly they have been replaced by tape, 8 tracks, cassettes, CDs and MP3, all in quick succession.

Or consider the retail high street and the competition it faces from online selling. The rapid growth of digital photography has seen the demise of shops offering photographic development. We are now seeing the next stage as digital cameras give way to mobile phones and tablets as ways of not only capturing images but also of transmitting them to social networks or storing them in the Cloud. Further changes are inevitable. We live in fast-changing times, which require fast and flexible change processes.

This also applies to software. Only 30 years ago, if I wanted to communicate with colleagues I would write a memo, send it to a typing pool, redraft and then send. This would take 2–3 days with a similar time lag for my colleagues to respond. Now I just send an email and expect an instant response. During the dot-com boom it was no good taking 2–3 years to develop systems – competitors would get there a lot quicker. Like me you may have friends and relatives who had brilliant ideas for new web offerings only to lose out because they did not implement and market them fast enough. Someone else got there first!

The same principles apply in IT and software. There are numerous examples where MS-DOS-based projects for providing desktop systems were abandoned overnight when Windows or MAC GUIs were introduced. Large projects that were set to deliver major changes for the organisation concerned often failed because they just took too long in development. Many tried to accommodate the changes in requirements, but this proved expensive and time consuming. There were too many runaway projects; I know of examples costing three or more times the original estimate by the time they were abandoned – with little or nothing to show by way of business benefits. Many of the runaway projects I have reviewed also failed due to lack of business input into requirements, particularly from senior stakeholders. A new approach was required and so the concepts of Agile project development were adapted to the world of systems and software. This started during the dot-com boom but has now extended to other types of projects including ERP implementations, maintenance and DevOps projects, and the Cloud and big data projects.

Agile definition

So what actually is Agile? Many organisations claim to be following an Agile approach and using Agile tools in different ways. You could be forgiven for thinking that the Agile structure lacks organisation and discipline and so is completely alien to the way that you normally work or audit projects. There are a number of definitions, standards and guidelines that can be used to provide consistency. The definition I favour, which is also widely accepted, is shown below:

Agile Defined

A-gil-i-ty (ə-'ji-lə-tē) Property consisting of quickness, lightness, and ease of movement; To be very nimble

- The ability to create and respond to change in order to profit in a turbulent global business environment.
- The ability to quickly reprioritize use of resources when requirements, technology, and knowledge shift.
- A very fast response to sudden market changes and emerging threats by intensive customer interaction.
- Use of evolutionary, incremental, and iterative delivery to converge on an optimal customer solution.
- Maximizing BUSINESS VALUE with right sized, just-enough, and just-in-time processes and documentation.[1]

This definition sees change during a project as inevitable, and almost welcomed. Instead of resisting or continuing to deliver as originally planned it stresses the need for flexibility and adaptability in the provision of useful deliverables. It does this by breaking the project up into smaller deliverables and ensuring full interaction from the business (the customer) in agreeing what is to be delivered

---

[1] Rico, David F. (2014, February). *Business value of Agile methods: Using ROI and real options.* Lecture conducted from Project Management Institute Washington, DC-Reston (PMIWDC-Reston), Reston, VA, USA. (*http://davidfrico.com/rico14a.pdf*).

and when. Users welcome this approach because they can 'touch and feel' real products and benefits rather than trying to interpret often complex and jargon ridden documentation.

The definition is widely recognised and can be a useful aid to auditors interacting with Agile project teams.

Critics of traditional, non-Agile project approaches often refer to:

- too much planning – emphasis on the inputs rather than the outputs.

- too little communication, particularly between business and project teams – relying on formal documentation rather than actually talking and listening to one another.

- lack of engagement, accountability, involvement and commitment of business sponsors.

- too much delivery in one go.

Agile tries to overcome these issues by breaking the project up into smaller deliverables.

Agile Manifesto

On a cold February day in 2001 a group of Agile experts met in a ski resort in the Wasatch mountains of Utah. Between skiing and après-ski they discussed the common elements of Agile and produced the Agile Manifesto. This was seen as a way of uniting thinking on the key elements for all the different approaches (e.g., Scrum, Extreme Programming (XP), Unified Process (UP) etc.). There are now a very large number of signatories to the Manifesto, and the list is still growing. The Manifesto is widely accepted as a basis for Agile (see *Agilemanifesto.org*).

The Agile Manifesto (see overleaf) is very useful when auditing Agile projects. It helps to emphasise the differences between Agile and other approaches.

> "We are uncovering better ways of developing [products] by doing it and helping others do it. Through this work we have come to value:
>
> **Individuals and interactions** over processes and tools
>
> **Working [products]** over comprehensive documentation
>
> **Customer collaboration** over contract negotiations
>
> **Responding to change** over following a plan
>
> That is while there is value in the items on the right, we value the items on the **left** more."
>
> *Source : Martin Fowler & Jim Highsmith. "The Agile Manifesto." Software development, 8,*
> *August 2001.*

Culturally in my experience auditors are inclined to the right-hand side of the list (process, documentation etc.) and developers to the left (individuals and product etc.). Indeed the characteristics on both sides could be seen as best practice regardless of what approach is used – the only difference is the extent of their significance to the project approach. We will look at this in more detail in the next chapter to improve the understanding between the two groups. But first let's consider the Manifesto in more detail.

1. People or methodologies?

There is no single methodology to ensure 100 percent success on any single project. Project processes and tools are useful to enable monitoring and reporting. Other tools can provide efficiency gains in the performance of routine tasks (e.g., sharing documents across the team or recording test results). However, projects never fail just because the wrong approach or tools were used; tools are only as good as the people using them. The skills, experience, knowledge and maturity of project teams will have a more fundamental impact on whether or not a project meets its objectives. Effective project teams ensure there is strong communication and understanding between them. Agile focuses more on the individuals and how they interact, both within the team and with stakeholders, than the tools and methodologies used.

I am often asked about the compatibility of Agile and some of the standard project methodologies such as PRINCE2. In my experience, it depends on how rigidly these approaches are being applied. If the principles are being followed in a general way then they can be compatible. However, if the organisation has strict requirements for adhering to these approaches, there are likely to be conflicts with Agile. There are a number of strong opinions either way on this topic, and the Internet contains many interesting papers on it.

2. Comprehensive documentation or a deliverable that helps the business?

To some auditors this sounds like heresy. How can a project really be successful without 'comprehensive documentation'? As an auditor myself I have often reported on the lack of documentation for projects. Let's face it, drafting documentation is far less interesting for a developer than writing new code or demonstrating the clever features they have created to a customer. As a result the quality of documentation is often poor. In practice, the documentation is not really understood by the intended audience and can often be misinterpreted. Even where it is good, documentation is rarely maintained, or even used effectively beyond the life of the project development.

Some documentation is still important, however, particularly to support major decisions made during a project, to provide work instructions to users or configuration information to assist with the future maintenance of the system. However, much documentation prepared during projects is just surplus paper. Detailed specifications and user requirements that are not properly written or read and are just filed for reference provide little or no benefit to the customer. They are more interested in receiving a product they can use to meet their business requirements, which includes basic documentation to enable them to effectively use the features available. Let me illustrate – you go to buy a new car and the showroom quotes two prices:

Option 1 – £15,000 for the car including a manual; or

Option 2 – £20,000 for the car, manual and a copy of the original design plans, development specifications, servicing instructions, wind tunnel tests etc.

While Option 2 may be of interest to some enthusiasts, most people would opt for the lower price because what they want is a car – not paper insulation for their lofts. If, however, you are an airline considering the purchase of a new super aircraft, you are more likely to want a package that includes the detailed documentation. The balance between documentation and deliverables will vary between projects.

3. Working together as a team or argument and stubbornness.

I realise I have paraphrased the Manifesto, but this is the heart of this issue. Throughout my career there has been discussion about the need for business and IT to work closely together. Yet when projects go wrong there is always an 'us and them' culture between the two groups – each blaming the other. The solution to this has been to develop service-level agreements and other internal contracts to agree the roles and responsibilities etc. I know that one part of a business cannot take legal action against another, but it gets pretty close sometimes. I have known some organisations where it is easier for the business to contract with external suppliers than with their own IT departments! Add in internal profit requirements and budget constraints and the problem becomes even worse. What the Agile Manifesto is saying is that there needs to be a <u>minimal</u> contract between different parts of the project team and <u>maximum</u> collaboration and working together. Agile depends on this level of trust and co-working across the team and is built on the assumption that mature professionals will all focus on the successful outcome of the project.

Time for one of my bad jokes – it's an Agile favourite. A chicken and pig were considering opening a restaurant together. 'What shall we call it?' said the pig. 'How about Ham and Eggs?' the chicken replied. The pig didn't like this: 'You will be making a contribution but I would be fully committed.' This joke is often used in Agile to explain the different types of players in an Agile team. The 'pigs' are those committed full time to the project. The 'chickens' are those on the sideline who have an interest but are less committed.

Question to consider: Are auditors Chickens or Pigs?

This raises an interesting issue for the internal auditor's involvement. Should the internal auditor be considered as an integral part of the project team or retain their independence?

---

4. Responding to change or sticking to the plan

Human beings are highly adaptive creatures. We flex our plans all the time. For example, when making a journey and our route is blocked we adapt and find a new route. When ordering in restaurants, if our first choice is not available we choose something else. Our overall objective of eating a meal is still met, regardless of our original choice. There are many military victories that have resulted from this adaptability to change. There are also many military defeats where failure has been as a result of not adapting to change.

So why should IT projects be any different? Many projects I have come across have failed because they are no longer relevant as there have been regulatory, legal, business or technological changes while the project was in progress.

The Agile Manifesto is saying that you still need an overall plan but it is more important to review and adjust this to the changes in circumstances rather than stick to it come what may.

Agile principles

A number of Agile writers and thinkers have developed principles to support the Agile Manifesto. They have similar messages and the common themes are broadly in line with the Agile Manifesto:

- Flexibility to accommodate change. Because delivery is incremental the impacts of business, legal and other changes while the project is in progress are reduced.

- Focusing on the bulk of cases rather than the minority (the Pareto 80/20 rule – 80 percent of effort being required for 20 percent of instances). In my experience marginal benefits usually have the highest cost and lead to project and budget overruns.

- Focusing on small component deliverables and the needs of the stakeholders.

- Fixing mainly time rather than other project variables.

The focus is on the importance of deliverables and the key stakeholders, who are more concerned with outputs than project inputs. Given the pressure we are all under to deliver more for less and the constant onslaught of change this has to be the right way forward, if adequately governed and controlled. Some Agile thinkers also discuss the benefit of doing less – this seems a strange concept to many, including auditors. The real point is that you are focusing on what is really needed rather than developing software where, for example, you could rely on standard software or tools, or a manual process would be more cost effective.

Three pillars of control

Agile control is often referred to as three pillars:

1. Transparency
2. Inspection
3. Adaptation

The first two pillars should be very familiar to most auditors as they underpin many areas of audit. The third principle can be more problematic, as it implies flexibility rather than standardisation of approach.

Transparency relates not only to the final deliverable but also to the process used to achieve it. Stakeholders need to see and understand the processes, terminology and standards used in order to have accountability for the outcome. This includes internal auditors. As documentation will be less extensive than for other projects they will need more direct access to the project team to be able to observe the process in action, rather than relying on a cold review of documentation after the event. This transparency will reduce the risks of misunderstandings, which results in poor and inaccurate audit reporting.

To an auditor inspection implies the review of evidence. Here inspection is actually referring to observation of both the process and the deliverables. This observation should be done in a way that does not adversely impact the process. To be effective the internal auditor will need to agree up front with the project teams how and when they will be involved in observations of project activity. Some organisations may have other separate levels of control review (sometimes called lines of defence) who may attend project team sessions and presentations of deliverables. Such regular reviews will reduce the risk of Heisenberg's Uncertainty Principle – that is, how do we know that what we are observing is what would happen if we were not observing it? For example, will the project team pay as much attention to controls requirements during its meetings when the auditors are not present? If the observation is seen as part of the normal process, the observer will become invisible and team behaviours are more likely to be their normal behaviours.

Adaptation of approach is a key part of Agile. Fragmenting projects into smaller deliverables only improves control if we have mechanisms for learning from mistakes and ensuring they are not repeated. If a Scrum approach is being used, for example, there are three opportunities for such a review of the process: planning, daily scrum and retrospective. The sprint review, or show and tell, provides a similar opportunity to adapt the current and future deliverable product. There should also be an opportunity to share learnings with other projects or programmes running concurrently.

As a risk and controls specialist I find this adaptability very exciting. I like being able to influence a project in progress rather than reporting after the event. On one project I made an observation about recording assumptions made so they could be shared with other teams working on the project. Within a few hours we had a mechanism in place and working – it was then shared with other projects. In a traditional audit approach this would have taken many weeks of discussion to achieve, by which time it would have been of little or no benefit to the original project.

Agile software development models

There are a number of common Agile models for software development; the three main ones are:

1. **Scrum** – Multiple independent small teams work intensively to develop deliverables.

2. **Unified Process** – There are a number of versions, based on the Rational Unified Process (RUP) software development process from IBM. It uses four distinct phases (inception, elaboration, construction and transition, and is business model based.

3. **Extreme Programming** approaches such as Dynamic System Development Method (DSDM) and Adaptive Software Development (ASD). These are derived from Rapid Application Development (RAD), developed by Jim Highsmith and others, involving a repeating series of *speculate*, *collaborate* and *learn* cycles.

Many organisations develop their own approaches based on one or more of the preceding models. It is therefore important that the auditor understands the approach being used for the projects they are looking at. The following description of each model provides an overview; however, there are wider variations in how each are applied.

Scrum approach

Scrum is currently the most common form of Agile development, so it warrants further explanation. The concept is based (loosely) on the scrum from rugby – the mechanism used to get the game moving again after play has come to a stop. The key features of Scrum are:

- The **product owner,** a key business stakeholder, creates a prioritised wishlist/high-level requirements called a **product backlog**.
- During **sprint planning**, the **team** pulls a small chunk from the top of the wishlist, a **sprint backlog**, and decides how to implement those pieces.
- The team has a certain amount of time, a **sprint**, to complete its work – usually two to four weeks – but meets each day to assess its progress (**daily scrum**).
- Along the way, the **ScrumMaster** keeps the team focused on its goal.
- At the end of the sprint, the work should be potentially useable by users.
- The sprint ends with a **sprint review** and **retrospective**.
- As the next sprint begins, the team chooses another chunk of the product backlog and begins working again.

You can see from this that the Scrum approach is highly flexible, adapting to in-flight business and project changes, and dependent on the delegation to an effective Scrum team. When operated effectively it ensures business stakeholders receive regular deliveries of product they can use – thereby achieving immediate benefits. In my experience the effectiveness of the Scrum approach depends largely on how good the teams are. For example, the product owner must have the knowledge and authority to speak on behalf of the key business stakeholders.

Unified Process

Unlike Scrum UP is used only for software development. There are many variants, usually simplifications of RUP. Although I have not worked on RUP projects I understand that from an audit perspective there is a library of standard documentation that is used.

All variants use the same four stages:

1. Inception (smallest /shortest step)
   - identify requirements
   - establish business case/scope, outline 'use cases' and requirements
   - identify risks
   - prepare preliminary plan/budget
2. Elaboration
   - identify architectural baseline
   - capture most business requirements
   - provide various deliverables (e.g., 'use case' and 'package' diagrams)
   - plan construction phase

3. Construction (biggest phase)
   - develop software based upon the identified architecture.
   - software built in short iterations – may be variable lengths – delivered software may be modules or components of larger sections of code rather than fully functioning on its own.
   - plan transition phase.
4. Transition
   - product is available for beta testing and is validated ready to deploy.
   - obtain feedback to refine deliverable.

The following table compares and contrasts UP with Scrum:

	Unified Process	Scrum
Planning	Follows a formal plan.	No end to end plan. Each Scrum planned in turn.
Scope	Predefined, can only amend in flight under strict control.	No scope – project backlog instead, reviewed at end of each sprint.
Artefacts	Includes vision/scope, functional, architectures, development plan, test plan, test script etc.	Documentation more limited – e.g., user documents only as included in requirements.
Deliverables	Each iteration may only be a component.	Each iteration is deployable.

Extreme Programming

Extreme programming is software development for the brave. Some regard it as the least structured but most creative model. The model is based on a number of phases, each of which must be completed before a decision is made to move on to the next phase. Each phase commences with a scoping of the changed direction of the project. Like Scrum the end customer is seen as an integral part of the team. Planning and tracking is kept simple. Teams focus on business value, delivering software in fully functional releases that fully meet all customer requirements.

Conclusion

Maybe Agile is not as anarchic as you first thought it would be. There are structures and tools that provide some governance framework. By understanding the Manifesto and principles auditors can tackle an Agile audit in a systematic and efficient way. Some auditors and risk professionals are going even further and applying Agile approaches to their own work and audits. The ability to be Agile does not depend on a single model or approach but more on how they are applied in practice.

CHAPTER 2: AGILE VERSUS WATERFALL

Overview

Having looked at the definitions and background for Agile, it is now useful to compare and contrast the technical and governance aspects of Agile and the more traditional waterfall approaches to projects. In this chapter we will:

- Compare and contrast Agile and traditional waterfall approaches for each project phase.
- Look at the risks and governance for Agile projects and consider how to audit Agile. This will include some typical audit objectives for reviewing the approach an organisation may take on an Agile project.

Comparing Agile with waterfall

The Agile Manifesto provides a useful comparison to the more traditional project approaches, and we have considered these in the previous chapter. There are other differences that are useful for the auditor to understand. These may also assist project teams when communicating with auditors. They mainly relate to the way that Agile projects are managed and monitored. The following table considers how the two approaches compare for team management, timing of work, governance and other factors:

	Waterfall	Agile
How are teams structured?	Different professionals work together but each has their own role – they complete their tasks and they pass on to the next professional for review and to complete their own work. This approach defines specific responsibilities but can be slow with delays between stages and lead to re-work and repetitive cycles.	All work together to achieve a common goal. The analogy often used is of a rugby team. There are still specialists who have a particular role but all team members work together to achieve the common objective, supporting and managing the team together.
Timing of work packages and project structure	Planning is based around phases of tasks – for example, planning/ requirements/design and then build. Each stage is completed for the whole project before progressing to the next stage.	Planning is based primarily around each individual deliverable rather than the entirety of the project. Some deliverables are dependent on others but most streams can run simultaneously.
Defined or empirical approach?	Defined with high predictability and centrally controlled. Always reacts in the same way to the same triggers and discourages change in flight.	Empirical as based on experiment, observation and continuous learning rather than theoretical standardised design.
The three variables: time/cost/ deliverable	Deliverable features are fixed; time and cost can be variable.	Time and cost are fixed; the deliverable features are variable.
Governance	Typically a centralised, command and control, same approach for all projects in the portfolio.	More delegation down to the 'doers' and encouraging and enabling the right behaviours and collaboration.

Another way of considering the differences is by a story. A king wants to build four towers and sets two teams on the task: one using a waterfall approach and the other Agile.

The waterfall team spends time planning and consulting on the requirements and design for all four towers before any work commences. When it starts building, each layer of all four towers is built before proceeding to the next. The team uses different trades to build each layer. All towers will be built to the same standard design. Each professional has a formal handover to the next when they have completed their own task. After 40 days the team has completed detailed documentation and is going through a process of agreeing and formal sign-off. Building has yet to start – it is not clear if it will now be achieved on budget as costs for the selected building material have increased. Also the project may be delayed as obtaining agreement is taking longer than expected.

The Agile team, meanwhile, undertakes minimal overall planning and then commences on the first tower. This is used partly as a learning experience for future towers with the opportunity for review and feedback. Each tower is an independent project in its own right. The materials used and the process of building may change for each tower based on feedback and other changes (e.g., the availability of alternative materials and change in design). After 40 days the team has completed one tower and work is progressing on the next.

In both cases an architect is employed to build the towers and ensure they are completed, using safe and effective processes, to business requirements. The overall objective is still achieved although the methodology to build the towers and the final detailed deliverable may be different.

We have looked at waterfall and Agile as if they are two extremes. Let us not forget the commonalities of the two; in both cases we need to ensure:

1. A useful product is being delivered to the business.
2. There is some accountability and governance during the project lifecycle.

Many organisations have a process that may combine these approaches. Even within a single programme projects may use either approach. For example, Agile may be used for smaller projects with unclear deliverables, whereas waterfall is used for larger projects with a number of interdependencies, and deliverables that cannot be changed – for example, to meet regulatory or legal requirements. To achieve this, the overall steps to be followed will be similar. Different methodologies, tools and organisations use different terms, but the basic steps followed for a project are similar. For the purpose of this book I have grouped the stages into the following cycle:

For an Agile project the 'Specify>Build / test > Give to business > Useable product' steps may be repeated several times, or 'iterations' as small incremental deliverables are completed and handed over for use.

There may be variation in naming, documentation, approach, approval, timing and performance of the preceding, but in principle we are still trying to achieve the same outcome.

In practice most projects fall somewhere between extreme Agile and extreme waterfall. I have seen Agile projects including more documentation, and I have seen waterfall projects where the design has been amended in flight. Each project will be different with different risks and benefits. Agile works best on smaller projects with a low lead time.

Waterfall is better for highly regulated projects with a high compliance risk. The best strategy for an organisation is to consider each project separately and apply the appropriate approach for that project.

Question to consider: The following are indicative of which approach?

- undisciplined teams/no team leaders
- no planning
- no risk management
- quick and cheap
- cannot track progress
- sure of success

Answer: NEITHER (or 'It depends?')

How to audit Agile/waterfall decision

The overall aim of an audit of the approach chosen is to ensure management is using the best approach for a particular project and has carefully considered the issues when agreeing an approach to be used. This will depend on a number of factors including:

- experience of previous similar projects and approaches.

- risk for the project including compliance risks.

- clarity of requirements or need for flexibility as needs become clearer.

- size and complexity, including any interdependencies.

- outsourcing or use of third-party advisors.

In my experience it is very rare to find a pure Agile approach. Most organisations prefer to have hybrid approaches. Hopefully they combine the best of both, but I have seen cases where they have had the dis-benefits of both approaches with none of the benefits! Combining can be effective, providing a good balance between flexibility and control. It can also be a nightmare where it combines the risks of Agile and the overhead and costs of waterfall. It is therefore important to ensure these issues have been considered in developing an approach for individual projects. The auditor should review the process that management uses to select its approach for each project.

If Agile is a pervasive approach in the company, being used for many projects, especially information systems developments, then it is likely to be audited as part of a General IS or Project Controls review. If there is a major project then Agile is likely to be audited as part of a specific review of that project. In either case there is a risk that the auditor approaches it with an expectation that controls appropriate to a traditional/waterfall project are in place. The following audit programme gives a summary of the audit objectives, risks and some suggested audit questions for each risk. It is provided to enable:

1. Auditors to have a framework to conduct their audits.

2. Project teams to prepare answers and evidence in advance of the audit, based on the sort of questions auditors like to ask.

The questions are suggested as guidelines only – the important consideration in an Agile audit is how has the organisation tackled this issue and is it reasonable in mitigating the risks.

The involvement of audit, or other risk specialists, at an early stage of the project will also help in the planning and timing of future reviews.

Objective

Audit objective: Agile versus waterfall

To ensure management has adequate controls for decisions regarding the choice of approach for projects (Agile/waterfall / hybrid) and has established the governance and infrastructure to support these approaches.

Risks

The main risks to consider are unnecessary additional costs, failure to achieve benefits or potential delivery delays due to management:

1. choosing an inappropriate approach for projects.
2. not exercising appropriate ownership and governance for the chosen approach.
3. not providing the correct infrastructure to support chosen approaches.
4. not ensuring the project team has sufficient experience or a clear understanding of the approach being used.

Audit approach/questions

Through enquiry and observation identify:

1. *How does management ensure it chooses the appropriate approach for a project?*
   * *Obtain and review copies of policies, procedures and guidelines for approach selection.*
   * *Ascertain whether the objectives for each approach are clearly communicated and understood.*

- *Review the mechanisms for choosing, assessing and reviewing the approach and consider whether this reflects the organisation's experience on recent projects.*
2. *How does management ensure it exercises appropriate governance and ownership for each Agile project?*
    - Compare and contrast management's Agile/non-Agile approaches for:
        - establishing and directing the project office and steering groups.
        - making IS and business management aware of their responsibilities and suggested approach.
        - monitoring and reporting progress.
    - Comparing governance approach to Agile principles.
    - Reviewing arrangements for the inclusion of risk management, compliance, regulatory, internal/external audit specialists throughout the project lifecycle.
3. *Does management provide adequate infrastructure to support an Agile approach?*
    - Review arrangements for selecting and training project teams to ensure they have adequate knowledge, qualifications and experience.
    - Review the management culture to ensure it enshrines Agile principles and the Manifesto.
    - Review the tools available to ensure an Agile approach can be applied.
4. *Does the project team have a proper understanding of the approach being followed?*
    - Obtain and review copies of briefing materials for teams (including induction packs for new joiners or contractors).

- Discuss the approach with a sample of team members to ensure they have a full understanding of the approach and their delegated responsibilities.

Conclusion

There are advantages to both waterfall and Agile approaches. There are differences in team structure, timing of work, flexibility to change and extent of documentation. The approach adopted for a particular project should depend on the specific risks for that project. For example, Agile can improve communication, reduce planning and focus on providing immediate incremental benefits for the business. It does, however, need to be applied effectively. Whatever approach is adopted the auditor should ensure their audit is comprehensive and the style and content of recommendations made is in line with that approach.

CHAPTER 3: WHY DOESN'T MY AUDITOR/AGILE PROJECT TEAM UNDERSTAND ME?

Overview

I can be rude about auditors – I am one. As a Certified ScrumMaster I can also be rude about Agile project teams. Having been in meetings where both of these tribes meet, it strikes me that there can be mistrust and a lot of misunderstanding between the two. In this chapter we will consider:

- audit and Agile cultures.
- how can we have a successful audit?
- Conclusion.

Audit and Agile cultures

The overall purpose of a project audit, including Agile project audits, is to provide independent assurance to management that:

- the project is being run with appropriate governance to mitigate the risk of cost or time overruns or failure to meet the project's objectives/key stakeholder needs.
- the deliverable will include adequate controls to ensure the accuracy and completeness of processing.

These aims should also be shared by the project team. Many organisations operate a 'Three lines of defence' approach to their enterprise risk management. This is summarised in the following table together with how these may be represented on an Agile project:

3: Why Doesn't My Auditor/Agile Project Team Understand Me?

Line of defence	Responsibility	Agile project approach role	Agile deliverable role
1: Business operations	Risks are identified and controls designed to mitigate them	Project or Scrum team	Project or Scrum team – stakeholder representative.
2: Oversight function	Review to ensure control arrangements are in accordance with organisation policies and other standards	Information risk management or governance, risk and control (GRC) team	Business' governance, risk and control (GRC) team.
3: Independent assurance providers	Provide independent, objective assurance	Internal audit.	Internal audit.

The anthropologist Edward T Hall developed a theory of high and low cultures to explain some of the issues that different groups have in communicating with one another.

High-context cultures:

- relational, collectivist, intuitive and contemplative
- emphasise interpersonal relationships
- need to first develop trust
- prefer group harmony
- words less important than context

Low-context cultures:

- logical, linear, individualistic and action orientated
- value logic, facts and directness

- solve problems by structured analysis
- discussions end with actions, often contractual
- use precise language

There are two things that strike me most about this:

1. Most of the auditors I know are primarily low-context culture types. They like accuracy, precision and certainty. They prefer evidence and documentation to harmony and interpersonal trust. Most Agile project teams prefer consensus and agreement and are focused on achieving a goal.

2. The Agile Manifesto we saw in *Chapter 1* reflects this cultural split. Generally Agile favours the high-context cultural issues rather than the low.

This presents some interesting challenges for auditors and project teams to work together. Both should have the same objective – to develop and implement a product with low risks and effective and efficient controls. The auditor should also not forget the specific risks associated with Agile described in the previous chapter. For an audit to be successful it needs to be seen as a team effort combining both the auditor and the auditee. This requires trust and understanding, right from the early stages of the audit.

There is a risk of a cultural imbalance on a project, leading to misunderstandings and poor communication of expectations. On one project I worked on testing was to be performed off-shore. Test scripts had been written on-shore and were vague and lacking in detail. The test writers had assumed the testers would have sufficient understanding of the objectives behind the tests and so would be able to complete them satisfactorily. However, the off-shore team was unable to do this and so just failed the tests. Eventually all the test scripts had to be rewritten and testing performed by a new team, leading to significant delays in the project. Management needs to ensure these potential cultural conflicts are discovered early and corrective action taken as necessary. If the project exhibits the Agile features we saw in the last chapter – in particular transparency, inspection and adaptability – such cultural issues should not be a major problem. This will help to avoid the risks of misunderstandings arising between auditors and Agile teams.

I have worked on projects where the project team was based in many locations and from different organisations. In my experience good communication and mutual respect can overcome most cultural boundaries, including those between auditors and Agile teams.

Agile works best where the project team has developed its own culture that works for them as a team. For example, where the project team is located in different offices, or even countries, this may include the use of videoconferencing and instant messaging to develop a common team culture and awareness. Some organisations also include HR change management techniques when developing Agile teams; for example, the use of Neuro-linguistic programming (NLP) to improve the understanding of team members of the behaviour patterns of other team members. The use of a team charter can also be beneficial. In Scrum, for example, it is common to see these including the five values of Scrum:

1. commitment to the shared goal or outcome of the project.
2. focus on the task and deliverable.
3. openness – promoting transparency.
4. respect for all team members (and stakeholders).
5. courage to commit to the project and share views with others.

Each team will present these values in a charter, and any new members of the team will be expected to work within the team using the charter as a basis. In this way the team becomes self-policing – for example, managing situations where individuals are failing to work to the standards expected and are therefore letting down other team members.

How can we have a successful audit?

A traditional approach to an audit would be to review a project, usually after it has been completed, and examine all the documentation. The auditor may work to a specific checklist of questions and will provide findings and recommendations. Given the cultural context we reviewed earlier, most project teams would not be comfortable with this approach – it seems to demonstrate a lack of trust. There could also be difficulties in that the project team may have moved on to other projects or deliverables. Any recommendations relating to governance may be incorporated in future projects. However, if the findings relate to project controls, it may be too late to make a change – and also expensive since a change process would have to be triggered. My top key tips are therefore:

- For high risk/significant projects audit should become involved from early in the project. It may also be beneficial to review a number of projects concurrently so that the auditor can identify and communicate examples of best practice.

- Using Agile culture, the audit team should ensure all project team members are aware of the audit, the need for the audit, how it will be reported and next steps.

I have used 'lunch and learn'-type sessions very effectively for this in the past.

Conclusion

It is possible for auditors and Agile teams to work together to achieve a well controlled product and a well governed project. The auditor can remain independent but does need to work collaboratively with the project team.

CHAPTER 4: PROJECT INITIATION AND RISK ASSESSMENT

Overview

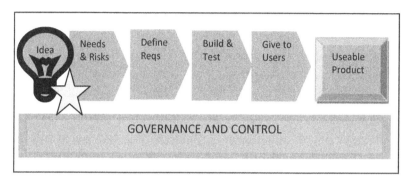

The initial phases of any project, waterfall or Agile, are important to set the scope of the project and ensure commitment from all concerned to achieve the desired outcomes. For Agile projects these project initiation and risk assessment phases are likely to be less formal than for waterfall, with the aim of achieving quick decisions and getting started on product development rather than documentation delivery. However, it is still necessary to ensure the project is desirable and will meet specific business needs. Given the use of Agile for cost reduction it is more important than ever to ensure the project is feasible and cost effective. In this chapter we will consider:

- project initiation.
- risk assessment.
- how to audit initiation and risk assessment.
- conclusion.

Project initiation

All projects have a starting point. Someone has an idea, which might be driven by innovation or the need to update software. At any one time there will be many of these within an organisation. There can often be more ideas than resources to complete them.

Given the flexibility of Agile it would be possible for large numbers of projects to start in different parts of the business with little or no overall business benefit. Businesses need to control where they use their limited resources, by considering whether these projects:

- have potential conflicts with other projects. For example, sales may want to launch a new range of products at the same time as compliance is under pressure to reduce the range of products marketed and their complexity.

- are trying to achieve the same or similar objectives or outcomes.

- could impede the business as a going concern.

- could conflict with regulatory or compliance requirements. For example, in Sarbanes-Oxley registered companies there is usually a 'no fly' zone around the financial year end, to prevent projects impacting financial reporting, going live and impacting audit compliance.

Senior management therefore need a mechanism to review and approve projects before they commence and then monitor them as they progress. This is the basis of project/programme governance.

The project team needs a clear understanding of what it is intending to achieve, and the business stakeholders need to agree that there is a business case to proceed. I was once asked to review a major digitisation project for a large travel operator. There were six major stakeholders for the project and I asked them all the same questions regarding the project objective and the channels to be used (mobile phone, internet, TV, etc.). All gave completely different responses. How can a project be successful if it is not clear what it is for? This needs to be agreed by the key stakeholders and communicated to all involved in the project.

A traditional approach is likely to involve a process of consultation, development of documentation and then a cycle of issuing drafts and convening meetings. The output may or may not be widely communicated to the project team and other interested parties. This approach can be time consuming and may take the project in a completely different direction.

The agreement of a vision for a project can be missing from an Agile project. Some project teams put the argument that Agile is about full delegation to project teams. In my experience this is incorrect. The Agile project team should have delegated responsibility for agreeing how it will deliver the product; however, the business and key stakeholders MUST agree the objectives of the project and its business case. To summarise:

Stakeholders decide 'WHAT'

Agile project teams decide 'HOW'

The best approaches for agreeing the vision for Agile projects involve short stand-up meetings of the people who have the idea and the stakeholders impacted. Using brown paper or one of the modern automated presentation tools, they create a business case, with specific, measurable, achievable, relevant and timely (SMART) objectives. Once agreed, this is then presented in the form of a wall chart on either a noticeboard or the intranet sites so it can be widely shared. Publishing in this way also fixes and agrees the project's objective.

Risk assessment

From a risk and controls perspective the project team needs to identify the risks associated with the Agile project and also make a case for including risk and controls considerations during the project lifecycle.

All organisations should have their own arrangements for risk assessment. In the UK and US these are likely to be based on the COSO[2] framework. At a strategic level the stakeholders will consider the risks likely to impact the organisation. This assessment may include political, economic, social and technological (PEST) considerations. Under the technological heading it is highly probable that the organisation's executive board will be interested in new projects that will change the business.

For any project, the auditor will be interested in how the financial, operational and regulatory risks are addressed. The same principles apply for Agile, although as we have seen the extent and documentation for an Agile project are likely to be lighter.

---

[2] COSO – Committee of Sponsoring Organizations of the Treadway Commission provides frameworks and guidance on enterprise risk management, internal control and fraud deterrence.

There are also specific Agile risks. The auditors George Westerman and Richard Hunter refer to the 4 As (see '*IT Risk*'):

- Availability.
- Access
- Accuracy
- Agility

The first three are generic risks found in a number of controls frameworks. Availability is about ensuring the system and data can be used by the business and includes disaster recovery and capacity management. Access, sometimes referred to as confidentiality, is about ensuring only authorised users can access the data and system. This will include user access, passwords, firewalls and segregation of duties. Accuracy in this context includes completeness of data and verification of data entry and processing, including key interfaces.

The fourth, Agility, is not usually included in traditional controls frameworks. Agility relates to the organisation's capability to respond promptly and effectively to change. Organisations cannot stop the flood of technological, political or competitor change – but they can, however, decide how they will respond. Organisations with low Agile risk are more able to respond quickly and positively to changes, enabling them to:

1. develop and sell new products.
2. scale systems and incorporate changes.
3. adapt their organisational structure.

The auditor needs to be aware of Agile risk to ensure their reviews and recommendations do not impede the organisation's capability to respond to change.

In a fast-changing world the risk of a project not being Agile can be as great as being too Agile (e.g., bookshops versus online as described in *Chapter 1*).

The characteristics of organisations with low IT Agility risk are that they are better able to:

• acquire and integrate new applications, products and processes.

• scale solutions as the organisation grows or shrinks.

• outsource or transfer services.

• adapt to changing customer market demands or technological changes.

An Agile risk audit can also help to identify improvements in the current controls framework and compliance monitoring process. I was involved with one project (C$8m) where the entire cost of the project was covered by cost benefits from reducing the cost of control and compliance. Monthly detective controls in more than 100 different locations were replaced by single centralised preventative processes and controls. Instead of teams of people producing and reviewing reconciliations before the submission of monthly reporting we introduced automated validation checking of data obtained from other computer systems.

By reviewing the existing ('As Is') control issues as part of the Agile project risk assessment opportunities can be identified to:

1. automate controls.

2. overcome any existing controls gaps, poor control or audit weaknesses previously identified.

3. ensure adequate controls are built into the product as it is developed rather than have the disruption and additional costs of building them later.

Improved controls mean reduced costs of controls maintenance and compliance. The best way to achieve this is for the upfront involvement of risk and controls/compliance/audit representatives. Input from controls specialists is most effective where there is provision for their involvement throughout the project. This could be via high impact, fun lunch and learn sessions. Yes, controls really can be fun. We ran one such session for project teams where we used prizes, games and music to engage the audience while educating them on why controls are important and the risks faced by other projects elsewhere and at the organisation. The sessions were well received and we were asked for an encore!

How to audit project initiation

Audit objective

To ensure management has adequate procedural controls and evidence for decisions regarding:

- project inception and choice of approach.
- the business benefits required and how these can be achieved.
- the risk/compliance implications of the project.
- phasing of work and benefits including impact on other planned changes.
- level of governance required.

Audit risks

The main risks for auditors to consider during a review of project initiation and risk assessment are that the project will not:

1. have adequate management of Agile risks.
2. produce a product that is feasible, governable or desirable.
3. complete on time, budget or to the quality required.
4. meet business requirements or strategic expectations.
5. facilitate ongoing compliance or overall risk management.
6. fit in with the current or future overall systems application and business architecture.

Audit approach/questions

Through observation and enquiry, identify:

1. *How has this Agile project been assessed to ensure specific Agile risks are adequately managed?*
   - *Review the formal risk assessment (e.g., guidance can be obtained from 'Risk Analysis for Agile' by Gary Mohan).*
   - *Interview senior project management.*
   - *Assess specific risk mitigations for adequacy and monitoring mechanisms.*
2. *How has this Agile project been assessed to ensure it is feasible, governable and desirable?*
   - *Review the feasibility study (does it adequately cover technical, budget, time, management and other change constraints?).*
   - *Review the governance plan for delegation to Agile teams, reporting and checkpoint reviews.*

- *Is there evidence of approval for objectives, timelines and realistic expectations/benefits?*
3. *How has this Agile project been assessed and approved to ensure it is likely to complete on time, budget and to the quality required?*
  - *Review the project plans and estimations if available (these will be at a high level for Agile as they will be finessed as the project proceeds).*
  - *Review team communications and interview key project team members.*
  - *Review project communications.*
4. *How has this Agile project been assessed to ensure it will meet business requirements and strategic expectations?*
  - *Sign-off by senior management, including key users and IS.*
  - *Experience of similar projects, including lessons learned.*
  - *Clear demonstration of understanding of an Agile approach and its implications.*
5. *How has this Agile project been assessed to ensure it will not negatively impact compliance or overall risk management?*
  - *Formal compliance review documented.*
  - *Training and awareness of compliance for all project staff (including SOX, etc. if relevant).*
  - *Authorisation to proceed, including identification of touchpoints, for risk and compliance teams.*
6. *How does this Agile project fit into the overall systems and IT architecture?*
  - *Does the requirement fit within the overall information strategy, IS service provision, and current and planned future systems architecture?*

- *Will the project create any technical or process debt that will need to be mitigated by additional projects and investment?*
- *Are there any restrictions or other general requirements that the project needs to include (e.g., standard non-functional requirements such as data structures, compliance with design standards or access policies)?*

Conclusion

In this chapter I have provided an approach for reviewing the impact of an Agile project on business as usual compliance, and considered how we can improve the operation of controls in a product deliverable (e.g., automated versus manual, detective versus preventative controls). The use of Agile does not remove the need to ensure there are real business benefits to be derived from the final product. The extent of the review is likely to be shorter and less formal than the auditor may be used to for other types of project, but the basic principles remain. The organisation also needs to understand the risks associated with the project, including any additional Agile risks, and ensure frameworks are in place for their mitigation. The intervention of the auditor, or other risk professionals, at this stage should reduce the governance risks and ensure proposed controls are adequate.

CHAPTER 5: CASE STUDY PID & RISK ASSESSMENT

Overview

The following case study is designed to help you focus on risk assessment for a project. While some of the risks will be the same for a waterfall or Agile-based project the case study also includes some specific Agile issues for you to consider.

You should review the material and identify the key risks that will need to be addressed for the system, and during the project, using the guidance in the previous chapter.

As with all case studies there is no right or wrong answer – instead the aim is for you to consider your response to the previously mentioned requirements. Your answer will be based on your own experience and knowledge; however, at the end of the chapter I have suggested what these may have included.

Case Study – extract of Project Initiation Document

Organisation overview

The Fore Large LLP is an international accounting and consulting firm operating in 56 different countries and with 5,000 partners and 100,000 client facing staff. Group turnover is $1bn and expenses are approximately $150m pa. It is internationally known for its high ethical and green standards. It has achieved a number of accreditations and awards for its recruitment and management procedures and has a very strong safety record. Unlike some competitors it has never had a serious investigation from accounting or fiscal bodies in the countries where it operates. As an 'LLP' it is not U.S. Securities and Exchange Commission (SEC) listed, but it has clients who are and Fore Large LLP has been reviewed by the Public Company Accounting Oversight Board (PCAOB). The partnership has hence decided to comply with Sarbanes-Oxley wherever possible as an example to clients.

It has grown by acquisition and has a large number of disparate systems that do not communicate with one another. There is a current strategy to improve this situation and to standardise on a single SAP platform. This is a major investment in terms of both money and management time. There are also a number of other significant projects to formulate global standards and policies, consolidate management structures and reporting, and still grow the business by 20 percent year on year over the next five years. At the same time the aim is to cut costs by 10 percent. This is to be achieved by standardisation of processes and systems onto a single platform.

Background to the project

An initial workshop was held to identify which back-office processes should be standardised first. The expenses system was seen as key because:

1. Every one of the ten original companies still has its own expense teams/systems/processes.
2. The existing processes tend to be heavily manual or spreadsheet based. This is expensive and leads to many late payments to staff.
3. There is a very high error rate at present requiring a number of reconciliation and exception reports to identify and correct exceptions.
4. The aim is to centralise the expense function.
5. The supplier of the software used in three of the ten countries has indicated that support for the older version used will cease in 6–12 months.
6. There has been an under-recovery of fees from clients as expenses have not been fully allocated to the correct client's account or job details.
7. The IRS in the US and HMRC in the UK have recently conducted audits. Although no violations were found there were a number of significant warnings about potential system failures.
8. To enable the later stages of the project, travel information such as dietary requirements and VISA information will be gathered at the start of the project for all employees.

There has been a lot of publicity around the project and it is being used as a real-time demonstration of the firm's

> adoption of Agile project management techniques. The firm's top 20 clients have shown particular interest in the project.
>
> The development of the software, testing and documentation will be performed by a third-party offshore.

Suggested response

How did you get on? The case was written to highlight some common themes and to prompt thought. Although there is no correct answer, based upon my own experience the areas I would raise are:

1. Reputational/regulatory and compliance risks are very high – even a seemingly back-office system could have an impact in a highly regulated market. Fines and reputational risk could fatally damage a firm such as this very quickly. By taking a stand on green and ethical issues it is even more in the spotlight. The desire to be Agile should not be allowed to overcome the need to maintain reputation and regulatory requirements. On the contrary the firm has an opportunity here to show how it can be achieved.

2. The integration of all the businesses into a single system can be a very high risk factor. Each will have their own ways of doing things. To adapt the system to meet lots of different processes could be very expensive. For Agile the key challenge will be to select business representatives who can represent all divisions, with the authority to make decisions. Care should also be taken to ensure local fiscal or regulatory requirements are not overlooked and can be accommodated.

3. Fraud and financial irregularity could be a high risk for expenses, especially if the system has control weaknesses.
4. Where there is a lot of change in an organisation management can suffer change fatigue. This can impact the ability to implement projects to the timeline required and can also lead to re-work where the project has not kept pace with the other changes. Using a proper Agile approach should help to reduce this risk and also the risk of technical or process debt that will have to be rectified by future changes and projects.
5. There seems to be a lot of different drivers for this project – are management clear on its specific objectives? There are good opportunities for process improvement and cost saving but these do not seem to have been fully evaluated. The timeline is also very tight – has a contingency been considered?

None of the preceding should prohibit the use of an Agile approach. Now that the risks have been identified it should be possible for the auditor or other risk professional to provide recommendations on how they can be tackled during the Agile project. Leaving them until the end of the project will increase overall costs and reduce the benefits achieved. Recommendations could include:

1. need for a regular review of higher risk areas by a regulatory/compliance professional.
2. ensure all key stakeholders, including audit and control, are identified and included in demonstrations and reviews of functionality. They need to take into account the eight issues raised under 'Background to the Project'.
3. high-level mapping of the As Is and To Be processes to identify the extent of the change for each major location.

4. ensure the right people are designated from the business and that they have the time, capability and seniority to represent the business on the project. Agile relies on this business involvement.

5. clarify and publish the objectives and a summary of benefits, especially if endorsed by senior management, to ensure all participants are clear on what is expected of them in terms of behaviours and outputs from the project.

CHAPTER 6: HIGH-LEVEL REQUIREMENTS

Overview

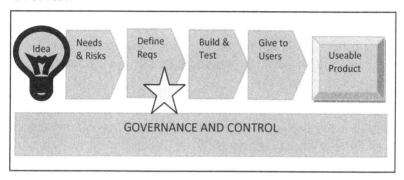

Agile projects still need user requirements before we can progress with development. But unlike waterfall projects it is accepted that this will be high level at the start of a project. There will be a general understanding of what the business needs from the project. Using Agile, we accept that this may change as the project develops; for example, due to other business or external changes. The full involvement of the business as a key part of the project also allows flexibility in the definition of requirements as more detail can be added as the project progresses.

In this chapter we will consider:

- how requirements are gathered and collated during an Agile project.
- controls input during this phase.
- how to audit requirement gathering.
- conclusion.

Gathering of requirements

Based on the project definition and vision it should be possible to start to gather requirements at a high level. Unlike Waterfall this will not be in the form of detailed design documentation. As we have seen this would restrict the flexibility of the project to respond to change and also limit the team's ability to be self-managing and creative in developing a solution (including business ownership and representation).

There should be some structured mechanism to gather and review requirements. The most common I have come across is the use of user stories (US) commonly used in Scrum or XP projects. In UP projects Use Cases are often used to collect requirements in business speak. The format is slightly different and they contain more detail than US, but they are still written in business rather than technical language.

The purpose of user stories (also sometimes known as Story cards) is to agree requirements of the feature that the solution needs to provide at an early stage of the project. They help to define and agree the scope of the project and to define priorities. This is so that planning and delivery can commence with some idea of the resources and other requirements.

It is DEFINITELY not to provide a detailed description of what the final solution will look like or how it will be delivered.

User stories may be written on physical cards. I have also used versions in spreadsheets and tools available from suppliers/the Internet. A user story has the format:

A <user role> is able to accomplish <some task> to address <some need>.

It may be useful to consider some examples of user stories:

- As a banking customer I need to be able to withdraw funds as cash from my account so I can go shopping.
- As a customer agent I can search for customers by family name, address or reference so that I can answer their queries.

The user story will be followed by acceptance criteria that help to define the user's expectations and will also include an indication of priority. For example:

I should be able to use my cash card to withdraw £500 in a single day from an ATM at any branch of my bank.

A good test to ensure the story is well written is to use the INVEST principle. This mnemonic was created by Bill Wake, in his article 'INVEST in Good Stories and SMART Tasks':

Letter	Meaning	Description
I	Independent	US (user story) should not have any dependency on other user stories.
N	Negotiable	US is flexible and can be changed or rewritten later in the project subject to approval of business owner.
V	Valuable	There must be some business benefit that can be derived from the US.
E	Estimable	US should contain sufficient information to enable an estimation of resource requirements.
S	Sized appropriately or Small	US should be bite sized – if too large or complex it should be broken down.
T	Testable	US or its related description must provide the necessary information to make test development possible.

I find the preceding useful when writing or auditing user stories. I also use the categories when providing feedback. Many authors miss the final testability requirement. If requirements are clearly written at this stage, drafting of test requirements at User Acceptance Testing will be much simpler. For example, test requirements can include tolerance levels, range checks and other variables to be tested, based on the acceptance criteria in the user story.

It is also vital to ensure good referencing of user stories. This helps project teams to ensure they can:

- easily refer and cross-reference requirements.
- identify ownership of each story.
- trace the story throughout the design and build stages.
- test all requirements.

User stories will usually be grouped into key themes ('Epics'), perhaps on business units, or common process areas. There may be common requirements across a number of these. For example, how data is to be structured and stored, management information reporting, release/security or compliance requirements or IS platform to be used. To prevent each project team having to consider these individually they will usually be agreed centrally. They may then be included in the requirements as 'Non-functional requirements'. There will still be a need to define any specific requirements. For example, the need for general access to be restricted would probably be in a non-functional requirement. The need for access to a particularly sensitive transaction to be restricted to specifically trained or experienced staff may be included in a business requirement within a user story.

Including controls in requirements

I am often asked how controls requirements should be included in requirements. This is a good question because if they are overlooked, it may be costly and very difficult to add them at a later stage. Business users or analysts specifying requirements may overlook controls as they may not understand what is currently included in the system they use or may assume they will be included as standard functionality. There are four main ways controls can be specified:

1. Create specific user stories for the control. This is useful where, for example, we need to perform a validation to an external source, such as verification of bank account details.

2. Include as an acceptance criteria for existing user stories. For example, a US for the input of customer information could include the acceptance criteria that data should be validated for accuracy and completeness prior to being processed.

3. Include as a non-functional requirement. This can work well if project teams have a good understanding of controls requirements, but can be too generic. There is also a risk that it will be overlooked during design, build and test. Examples might include 'There should be no segregation of duty conflicts.' This may not be specific enough for the designers and builders of the product.

4. Review proposed user stories/process design and add control requirements/acceptance criteria. These should include processes to ensure all transactions are captured and that data is accurate, complete and timely.

Having been included in the high-level requirements, controls should be subject to the same review process as other requirements. It is important, therefore, to ensure there is a clear and present risk that is being mitigated by the control requirement. The requirement should also be the most efficient and effective way to mitigate the risk and should meet the INVEST principles described earlier in this chapter.

The business representative (e.g., product owner) owns the design and requirements and so this should include controls. They should confirm they have reviewed risks and controls described in controls documentation and that automated controls and management information (MI) or other reporting requirements will be included in the build/test phases.

How to audit requirements gathering

Audit objective

To ensure management has adequate controls and evidence for decisions for the consistent gathering, assessment, prioritisation and approval of high-level business requirements.

Audit risks

The following risks should be considered in an audit of requirement gathering:

1. lack of clarity due to high-level requirements not being gathered adequately or completely, including specific controls, risk and compliance requirements.

2. confusion between requirements and design leading to restricted thinking during Agile development.

3. ensure the completeness of requirements to reduce the risk of scope creep later in the project.

The preceding often leads to poor execution of the project and business benefits not being achieved.

Audit approach

Using enquiry or observation, the auditor should address the following questions:

1. *What are the processes in the project to ensure adequate and complete gathering, reviewing and authorising of high-level business and control requirements?*

   - *Enquire as to basis for quality assessing user stories and obtaining compliance and risk/control management input (e.g., to see if replicating 'As IS' or seeking opportunities for automation).*
   - *Review a sample of user stories for:*
     - *INVEST principles*
     - *control /regulatory input*
     - *Traceability*
   - *Review mechanism for prioritisation and backlog tracking (e.g., to ensure compliance-specific issues are 'Mandatory').*

2. *How do the requirements allow for an Agile approach (e.g., flexibility during build, full out of the box and other design benefits)?*

   - *Interview key stakeholders to ascertain understanding of Agile Manifesto and principles. This will be at the start of the project but may be revisited as project progresses.*

- *Review key documentation and training materials.*
- *Review the original scope and vision of the project to ensure high-level requirements are in line with stakeholder expectations.*
3. *What are the processes to ensure requirements are complete and to control changes made to requirements as the build progresses?*
   - *Review sign-off procedures for high-level requirements to ensure all interested parties have been included.*
   - *Review planned arrangements for adding or removing requirements as the project progresses.*

Conclusion

In this chapter we have reviewed how high-level requirements are gathered for Agile projects. We have also considered how controls requirements can be included and have looked at a possible approach for the audit of this area. Through involvement at this stage the auditor, or other risk professional, can ensure adequate controls will be built into the delivered solution (e.g., in acceptance criteria or non-functional requirements). Early involvement also ensures the Agile project team is aware of the need for governance throughout the project. This is still possible within the more streamlined Agile approach. The aim, in accordance with the Agile Manifesto, should be to develop an understanding in the project team so that it will consider controls and governance throughout the project rather than having to rely on extensive documentation.

CHAPTER 7: CASE STUDY FOR HIGH-LEVEL REQUIREMENTS

Overview

I have seen a number of styles and formats for high-level requirements. This section provides some examples for you to consider and recommend how you would improve them. There are no correct answers, but I have included some comments at the end of the section. A further hint is that you might like to follow the INVEST principles described in the last chapter. Background information is the same as the case study material in *Chapter 5*.

Case Study - extract of requirements

> *Fore Large LLP*
> *Extract from Requirements*
>
> As part of the standardisation on the SAP ERP platform we are implementing the SAP Employee Self-service for travel expenses process and functionality. The first phase of the project is for the online processing of expense claims. It is planned that following full roll-out of the project to all sites further functionality will be added, including tax reporting and accounting and to allow online booking of car hire, hotels and flights. This document covers only the first phase. The overall requirement is to enable:
>
> 1. staff to enter expense details online.
> 2. expense claims to be automatically authorised.

3. payments to be made and all accounting completed within seven days of receipt of claim.

This document encompasses all the business and related requirements for the project. These will replace a variety of current procedures, systems and processes throughout different divisions of the group, both UK and overseas, with a single solution. This needs to be completed for some divisions within the next six months as the existing system supplier has withdrawn support for the version of the system currently in use.

The project will be delivered in accordance with the new expenses policy to be introduced from next January (further details not yet available).

Ref	Requirement
1	***Staff to enter expense details online*** All staff should be able to input their own expenses claims, for subsistence and mileage expenditures in accordance with their own local policies and procedures, based on local currency and tax rules. Access should be 24/7 and be via the company's virtual private network (VPN) with single sign-on. Intranet access may be introduced at a later date. The ability to delegate input to other employees (e.g., managers delegating to their secretaries) is required. [We are not sure at this stage how staff will submit receipts – probably scan and attach to claim, but not all sites have scanners so may also require a manual process]
2	***Expense claims to be automatically authorised*** Any claims under $200 will be automatically approved and cleared for payment. Any claims over this amount should be approved in accordance with local delegation of authorities and sent via workflow to the designated

	approving managers. The system should allow managers at grade 1 and above to approve their own claims. Staff can be paid expenses into a different account to their payroll and so will need to have functionality to change their bank account details in the system.
3	***Payments to be made and all accounting completed within seven days of receipt of claim*** Once approved all claims must be paid within seven days of receipt and accounted for in the local accounting ledgers – even if incurred by staff in a different cost centre.

NON-FUNCTIONAL REQUIREMENTS (NFR)

Category	High-level Requirement/NFR Description
1.	Need to comply with all local fiscal and taxation requirements, including all tax returns and submissions (including annual expenses tax return).
2.	It might be useful if staff could use their own devices/Cloud to submit claims. [Could there be some data privacy issues?]
3.	Needs to be compatible with Windows® 7 and 8.

BENEFITS REALISATION
For the programme as a whole, business savings of $20m per annum have been identified based on reduced agency operating costs when service can be off-shored.

BUSINESS PROCESSES
An out of the box approach is being used for this project – may require some changes to existing business processes to accommodate this.

PROCESS CONTROLS

There are no control requirements for this project.

EXCEPTION MANAGEMENT

Only exceptions noted so far are to identify where approvals have been delayed more than six days – not sure how we will handle these; probably just let them through to payment.

This document is deemed to include all requirements and no change requests will be permitted

AUTHORISATION & ROLES

Need role profiles for submitters, employees and authorisers.

MANAGEMENT INFORMATION

This is an online system and so has no management reporting requirements.

USER STORIES

Ref US01.01.01 As a partner/employee I want to use information provided by the firm's travel agent when submitting my expense claims. Interface provides accurate and complete information on travel bookings for each employee.
Priority: Mandatory

Ref US01.01.02 As a partner/employee I want to use information provided by the firm's credit card company when submitting my expense claims. Interface provides accurate and complete information on employees' credit card payments.
Priority: Mandatory

Ref US01.01.03 As a partner/employee I want to use the latest work plan/list of clients/cost centres to allocate costs. Interface provides accurate and complete information on all client codes that an employee can charge to. Should be able to download this information whenever submitting claims.
Priority: Mandatory

Ref US01.01.04 As a partner/employee I want to submit claims from any location and designate a deputy to submit claims. Should be able to submit claims via web, Cloud, or designate a deputy to submit claim. Be able to submit claims from own devices such as tablets, mobiles, own PC.
Priority: Low

Ref US01.01.05 As a partner/employee I want to be sure that my claim will be paid automatically after it has been submitted. Need online validation and confirmation and automatic approval.
Priority: Low

Ref US01.01.06 As a partner/employee I want to have claims paid to a bank account of my choice. Employee role should have access to change own bank account details .
Priority: High

Ref US01.01.07 As a partner/employee I want to have all tax documentation relating to expenses provided to me each tax year so that I can submit my expense claim. Individual annual expenses tax return or local equivalent available with all required information.
Priority: High

Suggested response

There are a number of challenges that will need to be addressed as the project continues. While in an Agile project many of these will be resolved as the project progresses it is important to flag them at this stage. The new system will need to consider the following:

Business risks

The document contains very little information on risks and controls for the final product. Also beware of 'Low' categorisation – it may be low for the users but high for compliance/risk. If risks and controls are not included, or likely to not be built, there is a risk in an Agile project that they will be missed and not included in the final software. I would expect the following to be included as acceptance criteria or requirements:

- What will prevent the same claim being submitted and paid twice?
- What about controls over master data (e.g., employees, bank accounts, VAT rates, account postings, delegation of authorities)?
- What validations will be performed to ensure data accuracy and completeness (e.g., mandatory fields, range checks, etc)?
- What about exception and control reports – (e.g., for reconciliation of payments, carbon reporting, regulatory reports)?
- Lack of a process for receipts submission is a concern as it could lead to error or fraud.
- Regulatory compliance should include anti-bribery and data privacy/protection.
- Have we taken advantage of all the out of the box controls described?

Project governance risks

Even though this is an Agile project, there is still a need for governance to ensure key elements of the system are delivered to the overall timeline, budget and stakeholder expectations. In this case, failure would impact the organisation's reputation as well as having business consequences:

- The reference to *'This document is deemed to include all requirements and no change requests will be permitted'* is definitely not Agile as Agile is based on flexibility to respond to change. This would warrant further investigation to see whether an Agile or more traditional approach is intended.

- The six month deadline could be challenging – is there a contingency plan? Using an Agile approach, it should be possible, for example, to identify the 'Must' requirements and ensure these are developed first so that at least some parts of the software will be available in this timeline.

- No controls requirements – REALLY! There are actually a few, and if they are missed there could be a serious impact on the company. An Agile approach does not mean they can be ignored.

- How will the company ensure 24/7 operation?

- Access security is unclear; roles require more detail, including any segregation of duties/access issues. For example, will staff with delegated authorities be able to see/change their manager's bank account details? This is often overlooked in an Agile project, particularly in a Scrum approach, as each team may assume someone else is dealing with it, or each team may actually have a different approach. Access control should have some form of central review and a clear definition of the requirement as an NFR.

- What about data protection, including archiving/off-shoring?

- There is no provision on the high-level requirements for sign-off by relevant management. Without clear ownership from management there is a real risk that the solution built may not meet the business requirements. For Agile to be effective there should be active and strong business participation and involvement at every stage, including the specification of requirements.

There is no indication of how the $20m benefits will be realised, or how much is to be achieved by this phase.

CHAPTER 8: BUILDING AND TESTING

Overview

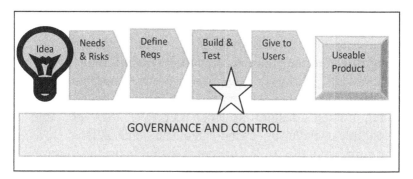

So our project has identified and agreed a need and we have specified high-level requirements. All that remains is to build and test and then the product can be delivered to the users. This phase is often referred to as 'Realization.

It is always cheaper and simpler to rectify faults immediately rather than at the end of the project. We need to ensure, therefore, the product is built to requirements and will meet changing business needs and user expectations. In Agile the involvement of the users in the build and test stage, and the flexibility to meet changing requirements, should help make this achievable.

For Agile, testing takes on extra significance as it gives the user an opportunity to play with the design and shape the final product. In this chapter we will consider:

- the build phase
- testing, including testing-led design

- how to audit the test and build phases
- conclusion

Build phase

In a traditional project writing code would not commence until all detailed design has been completed based on the agreed requirements. Developers feel comfortable with this approach. However, this does present problems if the requirements or delivery technology change, or if the requirements/design are incorrect. We then get into a complex cycle of change requests and delays. Just to remind you, the Agile concept is different as it recognises:

- the requirement/design may change.
- because we are constantly delivering small amounts of working product at a time, the risks are reduced.
- the full involvement of the business means changes can be accommodated quickly and detailed design finalised in-flight.

There are a number of common Agile development practices that may be used during the build phase:

- Extreme Programming (XP)
- Feature-Driven Development (FDD)
- Test-Driven Development (TDD)

As well as being considered an Agile approach in its own right, XP can be used alongside other Agile approaches for the realisation phase. There are five main features: communication, simplicity, feedback, respect and courage. The aim is to have a basic, clean but functional build with heavy integration of users and developers. This close working of the users and developers enables the detailed design to be agreed and built as the project progresses.

FDD relies on building an overall model of the final deliverables and agreeing the list of features prior to starting detailed design. There is more upfront design than in XP or Scrum, where the clarification of requirements is often seen as optional (referred to as 'iteration0'). The modelling approach of FDD is more specific and is included for even very small or simple deliverables. There are five basic activities in FDD:

1. develop the overall model – by interactive working.

2. build a feature list – usually expressed in the format '<action><result><object>'. An example may be 'Calculate the VAT for a Customer sale'.

3. plan by feature – agree and assign a development plan. Unlike other forms of Agile, code is owned by individual developers.

4. design by feature – groups of features to be developed in a two-week time-box are agreed.

5. build by feature.

TDD, sometimes also found in non-Agile projects, depends on writing test code before writing functional code. On one project I came across, the business had paid a system implementer to implement a major ERP solution using waterfall. After two years the business had lots of detailed documentation but no software it could use. A new small software supplier was appointed and they immediately tested their software against the client's requirements. No code changes were made. The pass rate for the testing was more than 98 percent, which enabled a rapid implementation using out of the box features, and the developers could concentrate on the additional requirements. In TDD testing functional code is broken down into small chunks, each of which is completed prior to starting new chunks. Different levels of testing may be used – but unit testing is always included.

Whichever method is used, during the build phase the main governance and control considerations are to ensure:

1. The product is being developed in accordance with the plan.
2. The final product will work as intended and meet the specified requirements (see the testing section next).

Given the flexibility of Agile it can be difficult to track progress as development progresses. In Agile, particularly for Scrum, this may include the use of story points and burn-down charts. Auditors often find it difficult to understand the concept of story points. This is because it is an estimate, made by the project team of the relative size of a user story. User story points are based on the Fibonacci series (1, 2, 3, 5, 8, 13, etc.). The sequence is the sum of the last two numbers in the series (1+1=2, 2+1=3, 3+2=5 and so on).

These story points are not fixed in value – you cannot say for every project 1 point equals 3 days or $500 of development time. Each project team will agree how many points it can complete in a set period of time and this is likely to change between different iterations as the team works together more. Points are subjective not objective – hence there is little benefit in comparing points set or achieved between different project teams. The underlying principle is that the team should contain people with sufficient experience and knowledge to know how difficult it will be for them to deliver the requirement as described in the user story.

How do project teams agree the user story points for each requirement? Obviously they play cards! 'Planning Poker' makes a game of the planning process. Special packs of cards are used and each team member is given a hand of cards, each card with a number in the Fibonacci series. The user story is read out and each team member then votes using the cards on the relative size of the activity. There is then a process of discussion, collaboration and re-voting until a consensus value is achieved.

Having agreed user story points, these are then used to track progress, usually on a burn-down chart, which measures points remaining over time. These are often displayed in project team work areas.

Being self-governing teams, Agile teams also get to define what they mean by 'Done'. Generally this will be the completion of build and user acceptance testing. However, in some cases, where for example acceptance testing is deferred pending delivery of other products, the definition may be more limited and relate to completion of user stories, including acceptance criteria, and unit testing. In these cases you may come across additional terms such as 'DONE DONE' and even 'DONE DONE DONE'. While this may seem vague to those of us who like precise definitions (i.e. auditors) it does provide a level of delegation to project teams. It is effective if all team members understand the definition and apply it consistently.

Testing phase

Testing forms an important element of Agile as it ensures the product delivered is fit for purpose and meets agreed user requirements. In highly regulated organisations, auditors and controls professionals may also obtain comfort about compliance of the product from testing.

Testing will be conducted at multiple levels. Terminology may vary between organisations, the main levels being testing of the:

1. specific product deliverables to ensure they work as intended (e.g., unit testing).
2. user stories/requirements to ensure they have been met (e.g., user acceptance).
3. integration of the product with other similar products (may be at a release level). This may include some form of regression testing to ensure no other functionality is adversely impacted.
4. regression testing to ensure the deliverable does not adversely impact other applications or functionality.

Tools may be used to track and report testing from agreeing test script, completion, quality assurance and resolution of failures. In my experience Agile project teams are not always aware of the auditor's requirements for testing:

1. retention of test evidence.
2. negative testing.
3. scenario versus configuration testing.
4. ability to re-perform tests at a later date; for example, as part of ongoing compliance monitoring.

For audit we want to see sufficient test evidence to allow someone else to re-perform the test, using the same sample, and get the same result. The easiest way to do this will be generally to capture screenshots of the test transaction including any messages.

Agile teams are interested in proving that functionality works. They often fail to test what happens if it does not work. For example, two systems may have an interface – the team will check this interface works as intended. But auditors are more interested in what happens if data cannot be transmitted – will bad data be accepted? Or will it be rejected and ignored?

Agile teams often build test scripts on scenarios – particularly for acceptance testing. This just proves the functionality works in one scenario. As there can often be many permutations of scenarios only a few are tested. Hence we cannot be certain the functionality will work in the same way for every scenario. For example, we may have functionality that says all journals over $5,000 are approved via a workflow. Using scenario testing, we may check a specific journal type for a division of the company for $4,999 and one for $5,001 to ensure they are treated as expected. While this is useful, how can we know from this that the values will be correct for different journal types or divisions? This functionality in most finance systems will be based on a table that sets the value for the workflow. A better configuration test, would therefore be to test how values in the table are used for the workflow and confirm the values are valid for each journal/division combination.

Testing can be seen as a deliverable in its own right, particularly if it can be re-used in some form in the future when changes are made or for ongoing compliance testing. This could include:

1. test scripts, scenarios and cases being held on team sites or other tools and easily indexed and accessible.
2. automated testing (rarer).

3. embedded testing whereby test modules are built into the software (even rarer – but sometimes see notes in code referring to tests and location of results).

How to audit build and testing phases

Objective

To ensure management has adequate controls and evidence for decisions regarding testing performed, and that testing will ensure management requirements will be met.

Risks

Product is not fit for purpose or does not meet user requirements.

Audit steps

By enquiry and observation, understand how the build and testing phase has been controlled to ensure the functionality and controls have been built as requested. This could include:

1. Is there a properly agreed and authorised test strategy and plan? Does it include:
   - volume testing?
   - user testing, including verification back to requirements as defined (e.g., in user stories)?
   - negative testing?
   - configuration testing?
   - performance across interfaces?
2. Does testing include regression testing of related functionality?

3. Has adequate test evidence been retained, to allow later review or replication of testing for future changes?

Conclusion

There are a wide range of tools and techniques used in Agile for monitoring the progress of the build and completing testing. As development is incremental Agile reduces the potential impact of failure at this stage as only a small deliverable product will be impacted. However, without proper control the speed of implementation and other factors such as the project team moving on to other projects may increase the likelihood of such failures. This can be a particular issue where the deliverable is not released immediately to the business; for example, if it is part of a bigger release. By understanding the approach to build and testing the auditor can provide a positive challenge to review the process being followed including quality control and evidence retention.

CHAPTER 9: HANDOVER TO THE BUSINESS

Overview

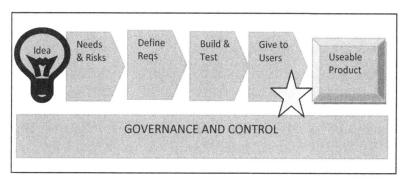

In this chapter we will consider the process for finalising deliverables and handing them over to the business. When an Agile product is delivered it needs to be implemented and used. One project I looked at, a hospital catering system, had been completed for two years and was not being used. The software had been purchased and installed using capital budget remaining at the year end. To be used, it needed further revenue expenditure to enable the catering department to input recipes and menus. They did not have the resources to be able to do this and so the system was not used and the benefits could not be achieved!

We will consider:

- how and why individual project deliverables may be grouped into releases.
- what the business needs to do to ensure it can accept and use the product to achieve the business benefits.
- what IT needs to run the product.

- what the controls and audit community need from the implementation.
- how to audit the handover of the product to the business.
- conclusion.

Release management

Agile produces incremental deliverables that can be used by the business. For small self-contained projects the product may be implemented and used immediately. However, there may be good business and Information Systems (IS) department reasons for delaying the implementation and grouping the release of software products together. These reasons can include:

1. The cost, overhead and disruption of implementing software in production (for example, it may be necessary to withdraw a frontline customer helpdesk to install a relatively minor management reporting change).

2. Business or process changes may be required before the product can be used (for example, a website may be ready to be used but the customer product or service to which it relates has not yet been launched).

3. Interdependencies on other deliverables/projects/business changes.

4. Avoidance of 'no fly zone' around the year end or other high risk event when implementations or major changes are blocked. For some implementations it may also be necessary to avoid month end or other periods of high activity (try implementing a new stock and delivery system into a toy manufacturer during the run-up to Christmas!). The use of Agile enables the project to be

broken down so that small parts of the software can be developed and deployed for lower risk areas during these times. This will reduce the time length for the project as a whole.

A release may consist of a technical IS code drop and a business 'Go Live' simultaneously, or the two may be kept separate. For example, any data migration or other business readiness activity may occur sometime after the programme code has been installed in the live production system. A formal Go/No Go decision is likely if the drop/Go Live are seen as high risk. For the full Go Live decision, confirmation may be required on the following readiness factors:

1. Code readiness and test results
2. User documentation and training
3. User role mapping (including assurances regarding segregation of duties)
4. Risk, compliance and control readiness
5. Data conversion/migration (if required)
6. Any dual or interim processing requirements

Business readiness

The business will need to make preparations to be ready for the Go Live decision. If Agile has been properly applied, the business should be aware of the impending change. The business representative on a project should be a strong champion to ensure the product will be implemented and used effectively. Other key stakeholders will have been included in user acceptance testing and reviews at the end of development (e.g., 'Show and Tell' sessions).

The areas to be covered will depend on the project, but typically will include:

1. awareness and training for both front and back-office impacted teams, including dealing with any objections or resistance.

2. identifying any software or processes currently used that can now be abandoned.

3. agreeing KPIs and other management indicators to provide assurance during the early stages of implementation, to confirm the embedding of arrangements and ensure previously identified benefits are being achieved.

IT readiness

The IS/IT function will also need to accept the new software so that it is included in frameworks for change control, IS security and incident management. This will include ensuring the new software is included in all backup, incident logging and change logs and complies with any IS requirements prior to code drops and data migrations.

Early involvement of the IT department enables it to:

- ensure there will not be an adverse impact on its own control framework.

- plan release and data migration activity alongside other projects and developments.

- plan the impact on the overall systems architecture and identify its own non-functional requirements for testing.

- prove that the new software integrates with the existing architecture and that it can operate effectively.

- prepare for Go Live, making sure any resources and service contracts are in place with appropriate service levels.

- ensure all systems operating procedures are updated, that IT staff are given the necessary training, and backup and disaster recovery plans are updated for the new software.

If the department has been given sufficient warning about the change, it should be able to participate properly in the Agile process. If not, it will be falling back on waterfall and possibly undermining the Agile Principles.

Controls readiness

During an Agile project, if the project team has been made aware of control requirements, it should have built into the system either embedded controls (e.g., to check data as it is entered into a screen for accuracy and completeness) or the reporting/workflow required to enable manual controls to operate. The aim is for the project not to adversely impact the control compliance of the organisation. These impacts could be due to:

1. inappropriately designed controls.

2. inability to operate controls after Go Live.

3. failure in the general IT controls environment that supports the system.

There may be benefits available from the software product that was not originally envisaged. For example, you may install Microsoft® Excel® to analyse data. The software contains additional features that can also be used to present the data in charts and so on.

Controls should be included as part of the general handover of the product to the business. If controls are not revised, the next time the controls framework is tested or audited it will fail. Worse still, failing controls could lead to financial loss, fraud or regulatory fines.

Whose responsibility is it to ensure controls are delivered and implemented?

A. The project team

B. The business representative on the team

C. The business/operational IT

D. Internal audit

Like most controls questions the correct answer is 'It depends.'

The project team is responsible for translating requirements and design into workable product, including testing to prove the design. Business is responsible for accepting the product, which may include additional testing to ensure requirements have been properly translated.

If there was effective business membership of the team (as there should be), controls should be seen as an integral part of the deliverable and hence included in any general plans for integration. This includes ensuring:

- control owners are trained to operate any manual or IT dependent controls.
- controls are documented in the normal monitoring tools and reviewed as a part of the control framework.

Auditing business handover

Audit objective

To ensure management has adequate controls and evidence so that functionality, processes and controls can be operated effectively and maintained by the business post Go Live.

Audit risks

The main risk is that the delivered product is not fit for purpose as:

1. The functionality does not operate in the live environment as intended.
2. The associated processes are not operated, leading to controls failures.
3. Controls are not operated, maintained or tested effectively.

Audit approach

While the audit objectives and risks for business readiness are broadly similar for waterfall and Agile, as we have seen the documentation and evidence under Agile may be different.

The auditor should ascertain the following by enquiry and observation:

1. Does the product operate in the live environment as designed?

2. Is there adequate evidence to support good control of the following?

- *Migration – that is, all sources of data have been identified and mapped with plans in place for controlled conversion and verification.*
- *Go/No Go – this will partly be based on test evidence, clearance of issues and bugs, and other proof that the product meets user requirements and stakeholder expectations.*
- *Role mapping*

3. *Do the controls operate effectively? Are the following aware of their responsibilities for the new software product?*
   - *control operators*
   - *control owners*
   - *governance risk and controls function*

Conclusion

By ensuring the delivered product is implemented and used effectively there is greater assurance that the desired business benefits will be achieved. Products not used are worthless to the business.

As Agile releases are incremental, it is necessary to ensure releases are managed effectively. Ideally software will be released as soon as it is completed; however, in my experience on large projects or programmes this can be some time after the software has been completed and so the project team may no longer be available to answer any queries.

The business needs to be trained and briefed on how to use the software and understand and implement any changes required to processes. The same applies to IS/IT as they will need to operate and maintain the new system. Controls and compliance will also need to take account of the change. By ensuring all of these arrangements are in place the auditor will be helping the organisation to obtain full benefit from the investment in the development.

CHAPTER 10: DOCUMENTATION FOR GOVERNANCE AND AUDIT

Overview

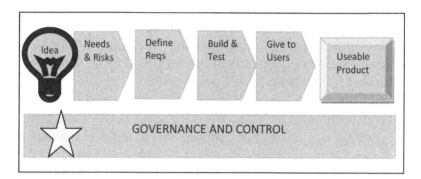

In this chapter we will:

- consider the objectives and principles of Agile governance.

- review documentation required to achieve these principles.

- provide an overview internal audit programme for governance review.

- conclusion.

Agile governance objectives and principles

Governance of projects is the control mechanism used by the organisation's senior management to ensure:

- The investments of time, money and technology into the project generate real business value.

- There are no undesired outcomes from the project or its products (e.g., major disruption to customer services, adverse publicity).

- The project can respond effectively to changing circumstances (e.g., technological advances, market or regulatory changes) while the project is in progress.

The first two issues are common to both Agile and waterfall project approaches. However, the mechanisms and tools used to achieve them in Agile projects will be different. The risks will also be different as the focus in Agile on shorter, smaller projects reduces the potential impact of any risk. The third issue is often overlooked in reviews of Agile projects, but is of key importance to ensure the Agile approach is adopted properly and not seen merely as a cost-saving exercise.

Control processes for waterfall are usually based upon centralised command and control processes rather than allowing individual teams to decide the most appropriate way to manage themselves. The same approach and methodology – and hence overhead – is applied to all projects regardless of size and risk. Traditional, often heavy, tools and methodologies are applied inappropriately. As we have already seen the focus in these projects can be on the inputs to the project rather than the outputs. Governance mechanisms are likely to be based upon time and costs rather than the quality of the final products from the project.

The assurance provided by these controls can be an illusion. You know the situation – project progress shown as 90 percent then suddenly falls back to 50 percent. Or when using red/amber/green (RAG) reporting a status is shown as green but is really a watermelon – that is, when you look closer it has a red squishy centre!

Many projects thought they were on track only to find they had 'runaway' by the end – leading to much higher than expected costs, late delivery and failure to deliver most, if not all, expected benefits. This has been particularly true for government and other public sector projects in the UK. In its publication *'System error – Fixing the flaws in government IT'* the Institute for Government makes a specific case for the use of Agile to REDUCE this risk.

Initial plans at the start of a large project can be little more than guesswork based on very limited information. Some of the larger ERP projects, for example, may run for many years and require millions of pounds of investment. The overhead of producing, reviewing and constantly changing budget and cost/time predictions can outweigh the benefits.

The National Audit Office undertook a review, in 2012, of Agile governance at a number of private sector organisations to identify examples of best practice. In its report *'Governance for Agile Delivery'* it identified four principles key to the successful governance of Agile delivery:

a. Governance should mirror the philosophy of Agile methods – only do a task if it brings value to the business and does not introduce delays.

b. Agile delivery teams should decide on (their own) empirical performance metrics they will use and self-monitor.

---

c. Senior management, external assessors, business users and the information and communications technology (ICT) team should be partners in quality, and this collaborative approach is an essential change in mindset. Remember that in Agile dedicated user involvement is seen as an integral part of the project team rather than an optional extra.

d. External assessment or reviews of Agile delivery should focus on the team's behaviours and not just on processes and documentation.[3]

A further Agile risk is to ensure all the individual product deliveries meet the overall requirements and work coherently together. This requires good governance and control of the testing cycles.

Governance documentation

The 'artefacts' or documentation for Agile will generally be short, specific and variable in format. As each team will be responsible for its own documentation, central guidance is generally briefer than for traditional projects. Documentation style and content may vary between different project teams within an organisation and also within a single team as it works on more projects together – hence showing it is continually learning and progressing.

We would expect to see governance evidence for the following:

---

[3] 'Governance for Agile delivery – Examples from the private sector July 2012' – page 9 & 10 (see *www.nao.org.uk*).

1. project initiation
2. project progress
3. project closure
4. product documentation

To allow project teams flexibility we would expect strong control by the project board at the beginning of the project; this is then to be released and then re-established once the product has been completed. As funding is usually approved incrementally, rather than for a large programme as a whole, the risk exposure is reduced. Senior stakeholders still need to approve a business case, but the format will be reduced and likely to be based on a summary of the commercial case for the product, specific risks to be considered and estimates of its value and costs to the business and proposals for tracking progress. We expect to see this formally signed off at the commencement and reviewed by the project board or its representatives at the end.

Each project sprint/cycle/iteration is likely to be short. A typical iteration will be about the length of a monthly reporting cycle for a traditional project. Progress monitoring may still take account of costs and time, but more significantly will track progress in achieving the desired business benefits. While cost reports and so on may still be available the most significant documentation will relate to this achievement and may be in the form of presentation slides, burn-down charts or other records of product backlogs.

Each sprint or iteration will contain its own documentation requirements. As a minimum, records should be kept of any meetings where prototypes are demonstrated to the business. Where additional documentation is required, for example to support business or IT operation of the product, this should have been specified in the high-level user requirements (e.g., as a user story or non-functional requirement).

Some of the standard features of Agile can be used for governance. For example, under the Scrum approach, we have the scrum review and scrum retrospective.

The review gives the project team the opportunity to demonstrate the features of the product to the users and other key stakeholders. From a governance perspective this is useful to obtain the views of stakeholders that the product is fit for purpose and will meet business needs. It also encourages future participation of these groups.

The retrospective can be compared to a lessons learned session for traditional projects. There are two main differences. Firstly it is held at the end of each iteration rather than at the end of the whole project. Hence any learnings can be taken back into the project rather than just benefiting future projects. Secondly it is a private session for the project team. Some commentators encourage a wider audience. My view is that this changes the candour and dynamic of the meeting and reduces its benefit. The presence of an auditor who has not been an integral part of the project, for example, could lead to a lack of openness and trust – this is against Agile principles. I would therefore recommend a closed discussion, although it is important that the project team can demonstrate it has acted on the issues raised during the discussion.

Audit of Agile governance

In the National Audit Office (NAO) report '*Governance for Agile delivery*', the CTO of Simply Business states:

'Auditors should not require complex metrics to know that Agile projects are in trouble.' This is because true Agile projects are more open and business representatives should be kept informed more regularly. Given the more limited documentation traditional audit approaches are likely to be too late and ineffective. To be effective in reviewing Agile projects audit teams need to rely more on observation techniques than on review of documentation.

Audit objective

To ensure management has established an effective and efficient framework for governance of the project, with appropriate evidence being retained.

Risks

1. Unapproved projects are commenced, without proper review of expected costs, benefits and risk impacts.
2. Agile methods and principles have not been applied, leading to the risk of an inability to respond to changes or meet business requirements or effectively monitor progress.
3. Quality and delivery are not shared responsibilities by all project members and stakeholders.
4. Excessive focus on processes and documentation rather than team behaviours – leading to repeated failure on later projects.

Audit approach

Auditors should not expect documentation to be produced just to satisfy an audit objective. I have had experiences where documentation was not available and so project teams have written it on the spot – I have put it into the audit files and it has served no purpose other than to satisfy my audit objective. This is costly and worthless as it does not improve control or provide real business benefit. Auditors should use interviews and observation whenever possible, with the aim of testing whether the product meets requirements and Agile principles/a reasonable approach has been used during development. Where documentation is required, for example as evidence of initial approval, they should keep a very open mind on how this is to be formatted and provided. Where there are examples of good practice the auditor should seek to ensure they are communicated to other projects.

Conclusion

We have seen that Agile governance is based more on openness and culture than on central control and governance. While this may make us uncomfortable we can see the traditional approach has not always been effective. By focusing on risk and awareness we can reduce the risk that a project will fail – thus demonstrating the Agile Manifesto principles. Which of the following is a real mark of success?

1. extensive documentation of what was intended and what happened during a project.
2. deliverable working product that meets the needs of the business.

Both together are unrealistic – I would prefer a working product every time.

CHAPTER 11: TOP TIPS TO TAKE-AWAY

When I learned lawn bowls I was told it would take minutes to learn the basics but a lifetime to perfect the details. The same is true of Agile. The best way of learning in Agile is through doing – being brave enough to make mistakes and willing to change for future improvement. There are five main take-aways that will help the auditor get started on their first Agile Audit:

1. Auditors cannot stop Agile – instead they need to adapt their approach and look at the benefits that Agile can bring.
2. Don't try to perform a standard project audit on an Agile project. It won't work. Instead adapt what you are doing and don't forget to also consider Agile risks. The audit will be more beneficial to your organisation if you show how it can achieve equilibrium between agility and control.
3. Be open in your approach to the project team – avoid checklists and standard questions. Use techniques and tools more in line with theirs:
   a. focus on behaviours not project process.
   b. consider quality of outputs as more important than documentation.
4. Agile provides some audit and governance tools of its own – use them.
5. Use the Agile Manifesto, pillars and definition when discussing governance with Agile project teams.

FURTHER RESOURCES

Books

Making sense of Agile Project Management – Balancing Control and Agility, Charles G Cobb, Wiley, 2011, ISBN 978-0-470-94336-6

eBooks

The following eBooks can be found on the Internet at low cost. They are generally self-published (except where publisher details are given) and dates of publishing are not clear.

A Quick Guide to Scrum, Paul Klipp, (see *www.paulklipp.com/resources.html*)

Agile Project management for Busy Managers, Tony Riches, 2012

Agile SAP, Sean Robson, IT Governance Publishing, 2013, ISBN 978-1-84928-445-5

Big AGILE Toolkit, Martin Leonard, v1.01 ix, 2012

The Elements of Scrum, Chris Sims and Hilary Louise Johnson

Lean-Agile Pocket Guide for Scrum Teams, Alan Shalloway, James Trott, Net objectives

Risk Analysis for Agile, Gary Mohan, *www.plainprocess.com*, 2012

Scrum: a Breathtakingly Brief and Agile Introduction, Hillary Louise Johnson and Chris Sims

Websites

LinkedIn discussion group: 'Agile controls and Audit'

PM Agile *http://Agile.vc.pmi.org/Public/Home.aspx*

Bridge to Agility (PMBOK)

www.sligerconsulting.com/book.htm

Agile documentation

www.Agilemodeling.com/essays/AgileDocumentation.htm

Scrum Alliance *www.scrumalliance.org*

Agile definition

http://davidfrico.com/daves-Agile-definition-notes.pdf

National Audit Office Report

www.nao.org.uk/report/governance-for-Agile-delivery-4/

Just for fun

www.youtube.com/watch?v=GE6YRc5XJVA

ITG RESOURCES

IT Governance Ltd sources, creates and delivers products and services to meet the real-world, evolving IT governance needs of today's organisations, directors, managers and practitioners. The ITG website (*www.itgovernance.co.uk*) is the international one-stop-shop for corporate and IT governance information, advice, guidance, books, tools, training and consultancy. On the website you will find the following pages related to the subject matter of this book:

www.itgovernance.co.uk/it_audit.aspx

www.itgovernance.co.uk/project_governance.aspx.

Publishing Services

IT Governance Publishing (ITGP) is the world's leading IT-GRC publishing imprint that is wholly owned by IT Governance Ltd.

With books and tools covering all IT governance, risk and compliance frameworks, we are the publisher of choice for authors and distributors alike, producing unique and practical publications of the highest quality, in the latest formats available, which readers will find invaluable.

www.itgovernancepublishing.co.uk is the website dedicated to ITGP. Other titles published by ITGP that may be of interest include:

- Agile Productivity Unleashed

  www.itgovernance.co.uk/shop/p-349.aspx

- Swanson on Internal Auditing

  www.itgovernance.co.uk/shop/p-1142.aspx

- A Guide to Internal Management System Audits
www.itgovernance.co.uk/shop/p-1542.aspx.

We also offer a range of off-the-shelf toolkits that give comprehensive, customisable documents to help users create the specific documentation they need to properly implement a management system or standard. Written by experienced practitioners and based on the latest best practice, ITGP toolkits can save months of work for organisations working towards compliance with a given standard.

To see the full range of toolkits available please visit:

www.itgovernance.co.uk/shop/c-129-toolkits.aspx.

Books and tools published by IT Governance Publishing (ITGP) are available from all business booksellers and the following websites:

www.itgovernance.eu   *www.itgovernanceusa.com*

www.itgovernance.in   *www.itgovernancesa.co.za*

www.itgovernance.asia.

Training Services

IT Governance offers an extensive portfolio of training courses designed to educate information security, IT governance, risk management and compliance professionals. Our classroom and online training programmes will help you develop the skills required to deliver best practice and compliance to your organisation. They will also enhance your career by providing you with industry standard certifications and increased peer recognition. Our range of courses offer a structured learning path from foundation to advanced level in the key topics of information security, IT governance, business continuity and service management.

Full details of all IT Governance training courses can be found at *www.itgovernance.co.uk/training.aspx*.

Professional Services and Consultancy

IT Governance expert consultants can guide and inspire you in the governance and auditing of Agile project management. Whether you are an experienced Agile project leader or an auditor, or other qualified risk professional, who may not have encountered this approach before, we can share with you practical Agile techniques that will improve your understanding.

With our help you can determine the most appropriate audit objectives, define the business risks covered by each objective, and decide on the use of suitable controls and how these can be audited effectively. Our knowledge of these areas enables the auditor to discuss the key issues, risks and controls for a project with the Agile project team in a practical and clear way.

We can also show you how to more closely involve internal and external customers throughout the duration of your project, identifying and removing any wasteful activities and increasing efficiencies in the delivery cycle through greater collaboration.

For more information about IT Governance consultancy services see *www.itgovernance.co.uk/consulting.aspx*.

Newsletter

IT governance is one of the hottest topics in business today, not least because it is also the fastest moving.

You can stay up to date with the latest developments across the whole spectrum of IT governance subject matter, including; risk management, information security, ITIL and IT service management, project governance, compliance and so much more, by subscribing to ITG's core publications and topic alert emails.

Simply visit our subscription centre and select your preferences: *www.itgovernance.co.uk/newsletter.aspx*.

Lightning Source UK Ltd.
Milton Keynes UK
UKOW06f1607050715

254559UK00001BA/40/P